Rafael Lima de Santana Santos

The evolution of Brazilian music criticism as a journalistic genre

Rafael Lima de Santana Santos

The evolution of Brazilian music criticism as a journalistic genre

An analysis of Rolling Stone Brasil magazine

ScienciaScripts

Cover image: www.ingimage.com

This book is a translation from the original published under ISBN 978-3-330-99752-3.

Publisher:
Sciencia Scripts
is a trademark of
Dodo Books Indian Ocean Ltd. and OmniScriptum S.R.L publishing group

120 High Road, East Finchley, London, N2 9ED, United Kingdom
Str. Armeneasca 28/1, office 1, Chisinau MD-2012, Republic of Moldova, Europe
Printed at: see last page
ISBN: 978-620-8-20080-0

ACKNOWLEDGMENTS

First of all, I would like to thank my entire family, mother, siblings, aunts, uncles, cousins, grandfather and Luce for their support; my father, for influencing me to learn and reflect on culture, and my godfather Joao Batista Santana, for always encouraging me and for being an example and inspiration to me. I would also like to thank my friends Ayslan, Keller, Kelvin, Luana, Marcia, Nathan, Sindy, Valter, Vida, Igor and Isabela for their support and for accompanying me since elementary school. Thanks also to my course mates Edie, Fatima, Helena, Junior, Lorena, Rayan and Sara, who became my friends, helped me a lot during this time and provided good times. I would like to thank my advisor Sonia Aguiar, for her availability, guidance and patience; and the professors who made up the panel, Thiago Rocha and Werden Tavares. Finally, I would like to thank the first person I met on the first day of class and who has become my eternal partner and my great love, my Juliana.

SUMMARY

The main function of music critics is to evaluate a particular production or artist, in order to help the public select what to listen to in the midst of the large quantity of cultural products produced. However, this role, as well as the profile of critics, has undergone changes with the advent of new technologies. Through content analysis and complementary interviews, this study seeks to observe how the music criticism published by Rolling Stone Brasil magazine is carried out, its view of Brazilian music and its role in the changing landscape of cultural journalism.

Keywords:

Cultural journalism; music criticism; journalistic genres; magazine journalism;

SUMMARY

Introduction

The choice of this topic arose first from an interest in the relationship between culture and communication and an affinity with *Rolling Stone Brasil* (RSB) magazine, but also from the realization that there is little research on cultural journalism, and even less on journalistic criticism in general. In a search for articles published or presented at academic events over the last five years, only eight works of interest to this study were found, four on criticism, three dealing with the first Brazilian version of the magazine and one analyzing the current version: Magalhaes and Santos (2014); Oliveira (2011); Fernandes (2010); Schoenherr (2005); Saldanha (2005); Bollos (2004). This research, together with Josd Marques de Melo's work on journalistic genres, formed the basis for chapter 2 and the presentation of chapter 3.

Culture and music reflect the historical, political and social context of a people. Several important moments in Brazilian history, especially from the 20th century onwards, were marked by songs that captured the feelings of the time, some of which are still remembered today. It is therefore important that there are studies in the field of Communication on topics like this, which help to understand the relationship between culture, media and society.

RSB is internationally renowned and had its first version[1] in Brazil in the 1970s, being a forerunner in the construction of a critical view of rock music. The current version appeared in 2006 and fills a gap in the national media scene regarding publications on culture and, more specifically, music since the demise of publications such as Bizz and Bravo. Despite its foreign origins, the magazine covers the Brazilian music scene in different ways, as well as other aspects of cultural production in the country. But the specific object of interest in this study was the music criticism pages.

In order to capture the characteristics of this activity in Rolling Stone, we opted for Content Analysis as the methodology to be used. According to Heloisa Golbspan (2007), content analysis collects and analyzes the elements that make up the media (texts, images, sounds) from a sample of the objects of study, with the aim of making inferences about their content and forms, fitting them into mutually exclusive and replicable categories. It helps us to understand a little more about who

[1] The magazine appeared in Brazil as a pirate version, independently edited by Luis Carlos Maciel, and circulated from February 1972 to January 1973 (see chapter 2).

produces and what is produced on this subject, as well as establishing some implicit cultural parameters and allowing us to investigate the organizational logic behind the messages.

Media Content Analysis (CA) is used to detect trends and models in the analysis of news cycles, framings and agendas. It is also used to describe and classify journalistic products, genres and formats, to evaluate characteristics of the production of individuals, groups and organizations, to identify typical elements, representative examples and discrepancies and to compare the journalistic content of different media in different cultures. Because of these characteristics, CA was chosen as the appropriate method to look at *Rolling Stone Brasil* magazine's view of Brazilian music through its reviews section and to see how the magazine's criticism adapts to the changing scenario in cultural journalism.

The corpus was then constituted by selecting the issues of the magazine to be analyzed. First, we took into account the time frame, choosing recent issues in order to obtain current results. Next came the concern to select issues in which there were a good number of reviews of Brazilian languages, which resulted in the choice of four issues published between February and May 2016. In these issues, the main highlights in the "Guide" section, including the front page, were related to national artists.

Before starting the analysis, there was a need to look for sources that would help the study look beyond the text of the review and to complement information that the CA alone might not have been able to reach, providing a better context for it. A survey was carried out of four critics (two who currently write for the magazine and two who wrote for the first version) and two editors of RS. We tried to get in touch with them via social networks, the magazine's website and email. In the case of the critics linked to RS from the 1970s, contact was only possible via social media (with the exception of Jamari Franga, who provides an email address on his blog). However, only journalists Andre Aloi (current critic of the magazine) and Jamari Franga (who wrote for the first version as a reader) got in touch and agreed to be interviewed.

Seven questions were asked by email about their relationship with music criticism and criticism by RS (see Appendix A) and how they see the changes that have taken place in the roles of criticism and the critic. The journalists were very helpful and the interviews were very fruitful. Their views served to confirm some of the concepts presented in chapter two and to counterpoint others. The analysis was greatly enriched by the variety of points of view presented.

Once the interviews had been completed, we proceeded with a content analysis of the magazine's review section. First of all, a floating reading was made of all the reviews related to Brazilian music, in order to observe the main trends in the text, in the selection of albums and in the critics' evaluations. Based on this reading, a table was put together showing the results of the quantitative analysis. This was followed by a qualitative analysis of the reviews, starting with the coding *of the corpus.* The raw data was grouped into units of meaning in order to gain a better understanding of the characteristics of the material.

The reviews were classified and organized, according to the proximity of their characteristics, into four thematic categories: the appreciation of established and respected artists in the Brazilian music scene; the new names that make a difference in the current music scene; a non-obvious treatment of traditional Brazilian genres; and the approach to products with less commercial potential. Based on this classification, a reflection was made on the stance of the magazine and the critics in relation to the national music scene, and the transformations brought about in the relationship between critic, reader and artist by the new digital technologies, seeking to contextualize the observations with the concepts presented in academic research and with the view given by the critics interviewed.

1 - Cultural criticism as a journalistic genre

Cultural criticism emerged as a way of appreciating works of traditional artistic manifestations (plastic arts, music, literature, theater). It was aimed at a restricted audience that formed the social and cultural elite. With industrialization and the massification of journalism, criticism began to deal with the products of the cultural industry[2] . The genre moves from an aesthetic character, which aims to analyze the work of art in depth, to the *review* format, which makes a more simplified analysis of a given cultural product, reaching a large, heterogeneous audience with very different interests. Jose Marques de Melo defines the review as:

> A journalistic genre designed to guide the public in their choice of cultural products circulating on the market. It is not intended to offer an aesthetic judgment, but rather to give a light appraisal, without going into its essence as a cultural good. It is an eminently utilitarian activity; since there are many options on the cultural market, consumers want to have information and value judgments to help them make a purchasing decision (MELO, 2003, p. 132).

In this way, journalistic criticism takes on the role of helping the public to become aware of what is being produced by the cultural industry and to select what *is* relevant in an increasingly vast and diverse cultural scene, which is expanding at high speed with the advance of digital technologies.

According to Rafael Schoenherr (2005, p. 8), the critic, at first:

> He is the specialist in digging up the world of music, an expert on whom readers place (some) trust. Under these conditions, this professional also has legitimacy when he follows the most diverse events in the cultural field in a more systematic way.

There is disagreement between authors as to the classification of types of criticism. Melo (2003) highlights two main types pointed out by Todd Hunt: the first *is* historical criticism, which judges works based on a contextualization of what has been produced previously; the second is impressionist criticism, which judges based on the critic's reaction and impressions of the work. The standard North American review (used by RS) is a combination of these two types. First there is a brief analysis of precedents, placing the work in a historical, aesthetic or political context;

---

[2]A concept coined by Theodor Adorno and Max Horkheimer (1947) to designate the industries of entertainment and the dissemination of cultural-symbolic goods, generally broadcast by radio, television, newspapers, magazines, cinema, etc. (Brittos and Miguel, 2010).

then there is the appreciation of the work with its positive and negative points; and finally, the conclusion, which gives the critic's final impression of the work analyzed. This pattern is also widely used in Brazil.

Cassiano de Oliveira discusses the role of critics in the music industry, citing various authors, including Mark Fenster, who considers that critics have both the function of opinion formers and that of capitalist workers. They represent their loyal audience by disseminating information about songs and their opinions to the media market. The author discusses the commercial nature of music and of publications aimed at covering music:

> The commercial nature of the music and publishing industries structures the possible content of music journalism and criticism. Speaking from a discursive and economic position within the institutions of mass culture, popular music critics and journalists judge recordings, live performances, music news, current events and the lives of artists according to a certain circle of evaluation for consumers. The questions that a buyer of a publication like Rolling Stone and Spin (as opposed to market publications like Billboard) asks and tries to answer are: Should you buy that record? Should you go to that concert? Is this guy an idiot and, therefore, should I like and buy more or less of his music? Music criticism has recently been at the center of the role of popular music in a consumer society (FENSTER, 2002, apud OLIVEIRA, 2011, p. 55).

Oliveira complements Roy Shuker's opinion that music magazines act in the popular music industry, motivating readers to buy recordings and all kinds of music-related products, and end up having themselves as consumers of 'pop' culture. Similarly, music critics act as service providers for the music industry, stimulating the desire for both to buy new products and to revere those that are considered classics. In this way, both the press and the critics play an ideological role.

> They distance themselves as consumers of popular music from the fact that they are buying a 'commodity', through the pressure of a significant cultural product. Furthermore, this function is supported by the important point that the music press is not, in a direct way, vertically integrated into the music industry (i.e. belonging to the record labels). A sense of distance is thus maintained while, at the same time, the industry's constant need to sell new images, styles and products is met (Shuker, 2000, apud Oliveira, 2011, p. 55).

In the current Brazilian scenario, this distance between the press and record companies doesn't always apply, since there are cases in which some media outlets and record companies are part of the same conglomerate, as in the case of the Globo organizations, which not only control a significant part of the national hegemonic media, but also own the Som Livre record company.

Criticism has the classic conception of mediating between author/work and audience. However, it also takes on the task of "formulating, on behalf of the public, questions that perhaps not even the public knows how to ask, as well as providing the answers" (Vasconcelos, 2000, apud Schoenherr, 2005, p. 2). In the case of music criticism, there are flow relations between the producer system (products, shows, artists, record companies), the user (listeners, readers, consumers, fans...) - which today is called the "music production chain" - and the feedback system, to which journalistic criticism belongs.

In other words, journalistic criticism is both feedback on cultural production and media production, which also has its own feedback subsystem. The difference between the feedback provided by criticism is that it allows for feedback from a wide and diverse audience, with a greater variety of perspectives and a broader cross-section of society. It is therefore a mediatized social interaction.

1.1. Music criticism in Brazil

The interaction between a phonographic product, journalistic criticism and its readers differs over time and space. In Brazil, criticism was focused only on classical music and was written by specialized writers. At the end of the 1950s, with the birth of Bossa Nova[3] , it began to deal with popular music and took on the form of a review. Liliana Harb Bollos (2004) points out that this new format imposed changes on music criticism, as it was produced by journalists and explored a more ideological and historical character and a less static one, leaving the musical aspects in the background. After the rise of Bossa Nova, two groups of music critics formed: the first sought to interpret Bossa Nova without imposing their personal taste; the second showed a hostile attitude to the movement, without proposing an interpretation of the work.

This fact was considered negative by the author because it created an obstacle

[3] A Brazilian musical movement originated in Rio de Janeiro in 1958 by singer-songwriter Joao Gilberto, which was a watershed in Brazilian music and led to names like Tom Jobim and Vinicius de Moraes, major influences to this day.

to understanding the Brazilian musical repertoire, since "the aim of journalistic criticism is to be able to identify the artist's project by analyzing the work, enabling it to be disseminated and assimilated by other people" (BOLLOS, 2004, p. 272). From this perspective, the critic should not simply take a position for or against the object; the critic must have, above their personal taste, knowledge of what is being debated.

According to Oliveira (2011), from the 1970s onwards, with the emergence of specialized music magazines, music criticism became more democratic in the sense that it covered more musical genres, such as rock and pop, and was no longer restricted to MPB[4] . Fernanda Pires Alvarenga Fernandes (2010) points out that the 1980s saw a widening of the interface between the press and the Cultural Industry, in journalism that also became more technological, fragmented and fast-paced. The first version of Rolling Stone Brasil was responsible for paving the way. This was followed by publications that helped to promote a greater professionalization of criticism, such as the magazines Somtres (1979-1989) and Bizz/Showbizz (1985-2001).

Somtres was the first magazine to address a wider audience, which consumed not only music genres such as rock, both domestic and foreign, but also Brazilian popular music, jazz, classical music and disco. It focused on the relationship between radio and TV and the world of music and sought to highlight artists and groups ignored by the media. Another important feature is that the magazine not only evaluated the songs on an LP[5] , but also the sound quality of the product. Oliveira (2011) points to Somtres as an important vehicle for analyzing the rise of Brazilian rock in the 1980s.

Bizz/Showbizz is considered by many to be the most important music publication to have circulated in the Pacific due to its reach and longevity. It was the first magazine up to that point to include not journalists, but musicians (linked to journalism) as critics. Rafael Machado Saldanha (2005) points out that Bizz played a major role in shaping the readership of rock magazines, setting the standards for what the public is looking for in today's publications.

---

[4] An acronym for Brazilian popular music used to refer to the musical genre that emerged in the 1960s as a manifestation against the military dictatorship, revealing names such as Chico Buarque and Caetano Veloso and today also encompasses later artists who follow the style they created.

[5] Acronym for Long Play, a vinyl-based medium developed at the end of the 1940s for music reproduction.

Oliveira (2011) states that the profile of the magazine's critics has changed over the years. From 1988 onwards, a more radical tone was adopted, which at times went beyond journalism. With its editorial reform in the 1990s, there was a softening with the introduction of qualified names to the team. In 1998, a strong nostalgic content prevailed in editorial terms. There was a strong insurgence of groups from the 1980s, who would look to musical proposals from the past to reinsert themselves into the market. All these changes were trends that were reflected in the rest of the media, in other words, the magazine's criticism reflected the dominant thinking in the Brazilian music scene at that time.

1.2. Expansion and transformations of criticism

With the expansion of the cultural industry in Brazil and the growth of the consumer public for cultural products, the scope of criticism as a journalistic genre has widened. It is no longer limited to printed newspapers and magazines, but also includes radio, television, the Internet and zines. This scenario raises a number of questions, because at the same time as there is this expansion in the use of the review, there is also the wear and tear caused by this growth in activity, which is not always done in a systematic, elucidative or creative way. This precariousness is largely responsible for the public devaluation of the role of the critic in the country (Schoenherr, 2005). In this sense, Schoenherr proposes a reflection on the tense relationship between criticism and the cultural scene as a whole.

> Critics experience dramas between information and formation, between being ephemeral or lasting, between transience and consistency, specialization and generality, opinion and information, the personal and the collective. The critic is (in a duel) between the amateur and the professional, the musician and the journalist (in our case). In what he focuses on, he reveals a tremolo between the national and the international, the close and the distant, the popular and the erudite, the past and the urgent, the manufactured and the spontaneous, and other oppositions capable of swaying judgment (Schoenherr, 2005, p. 6).

For Fernanda Pires Alvarenga Fernandes (2010), cultural journalism and especially criticism have three basic functions: to guide readers, to discuss and to help artists evaluate their work. To do this, the critic needs to analyze the structure of the work and provide a complement, reconciling reflection with objectivity and clarity, although this task doesn't always require objective criteria, but rather poetic and metaphorical ones. This makes impartiality in criticism a myth, after all, critical judgment depends on certain preconceptions. However, critics have not used this freedom of opinion to create discussions in the intellectual environment, generating a "de-intellectualization" of the function.

Many of these professionals take an incisive judgmental stance, holding a concentration of power capable of glorifying or destroying. This practice ends up distorting the role of criticism and only serves to boost the ego of its practitioners. Another danger is the exaggerated partiality of the opinion, when there is a difference in the treatment given to friends or works with which the critic has more affinity, adopting a more tolerant stance, and total severity towards disaffected people or products with which he has no closeness.

The role of criticism, when done well, should be to foster a great deal of interaction between musicians, readers and journalists about music. In the media, you come into contact with a different interpretation of a given product and, socially, you promote position reviews, confrontations, agreement, acceptance and response. As Schoenherr (2005) states, journalistic criticism gradually builds up a set of interpretations about contemporary cultural production based on objective arguments and observations, but also influenced by personal impressions and experiences.

Criticism promotes a broad social reading of the cultural production of a time. The object of criticism relates to previous and contemporary works by the artist himself and others. In this way, "individual reading is also social, because it takes place under specific cultural and historical conditions" (Nunes, 2000, apud Schoenherr 2005, p. 11). Based on this, Schoenherr (2005) establishes the reading of the review as a *social practice.* This process goes beyond the individual reaction of readers and brings together a variety of interpretations and views on musical products. This conversation promotes learning between artist, critic and audience. Criticism must work with mistakes and successes in favor of a diverse and productive participation in cultural products.

Cultural criticism, as an opinionated journalistic genre, has the capacity to intervene in the music industry. It can happen in a variety of ways, such as by highlighting a cultural fact; by questioning an established and officialized truth, as well as its naturalization by common sense; by promoting a debate on pertinent issues at the time; by exposing new paths, new visions and alternatives to the current cultural standard, among others. Criticism, together with cultural journalism, should be questioning, should provoke debate, problematize issues and not just report passively. "In journalism, criticism has the singularity of lending itself precisely to evaluation, to the opinionated aspect of criticality, much more than other spheres, which are much more tied to informative logic" (SCHOENHERR, 2005, p. 13).

2 - Music review in Rolling Stone Brasil magazine

Rolling Stone magazine (RS) was founded in the United States by Jann S. Werner in 1967. It began as an *underground publication,* focused on everything related to the counter-culture movements that were on the rise among young people at the time. The magazine was the first to feature major articles dedicated to pop culture and youth culture. Oliveira (2011) quotes a statement by Werner about the aim of the publication:

> From the outset, we have tried to operate on a very solid, very commercial basis. We also want to make money. We're in business, we're not ashamed of it, and we're about music. Music is the most definable part of youth culture, it's the thing that most people are interested in and, more importantly, it was the method of communicating people (WENNER apud Oliveira, 2011, m p. 218).

Along these lines, the magazine was very successful and was soon adapted for other countries such as England, Germany, France, Italy, Australia, Argentina and Brazil. This expansion was a reflection of the growing globalization of popular music, as well as the predominance of American artists.

In Brazil, the first version of Rolling Stone was published independently by Luis Carlos Maciel (a pioneer in the dissemination of counter-cultural ideas in the Brazilian press) and was considered a "pirate" version. It had 36 issues published between February 1, 1972 and January 5, 1973. It was first published fortnightly, and from July onwards, weekly. It also focused on counterculture, the *underground* scene and young people, with rock music as its main focus.

The magazine circulated during the harshest period of the military dictatorship, with a lot of political, behavioral and cultural repression and strong censorship of customs outside the conservative standard, such as counterculture. In addition, the military regime's policies prevented the expansion of the record market to the immediate benefit of so-called Brazilian popular music. At the same time, it created the conditions for the large multinational companies in the sector or their representatives established in the country to respond to this expanding market with a growing number of foreign languages. This scenario greatly influenced RS's approach to Brazilian music.

In his analysis of the editions of this phase of the magazine, Oliveira (2011) found that the number of music reviews and reports on Brazilian groups and artists was low. Perhaps this was due to the precariousness of the publication. Under these conditions, RS was fighting a phenomenon that was characteristic of Brazil in the 1970s: the emergence of artists and groups who sang in English and adopted pseudonyms, passing themselves off as foreign artists. Something that also had to do with the context of the time, the overvaluation of the United States as a world power, stimulated by the military and by part of the Brazilian industrial bourgeoisie, including culture and the *American way of life.*

The author observes that these groups and artists, as well as creating a false vision of pop music, unleashed a clear process that mixed acculturation with marketing opportunism. The magazine completely rejected the musical style adopted by these groups. "As well as being questionable from the point of view of credibility, the musical style had, for the most part, melodies based on foreign *hits of* the time, with no relation to other musical movements aimed at the youth culture of the time" (OLIVEIRA, 2011, p. 77-78). The influence of foreign music on Brazilian music was also a subject frequently addressed in the publication's texts.

The reviews in this first version of RSB analyzed records and concerts and were divided into three columns: Discos, RS Recomenda and Toque, which was the main one, written by journalist Ezequiel Neves. Oliveira (2011) classified the critic's text as restless, irreverent and sarcastic, just like his personality. He also shows the difficulties of practicing the profession at the time, due to problems such as the amateurishness of the record companies' publicity departments. Criticism was not restricted to rock and pop music. Artists such as Roberto Carlos and Agnaldo Timoteo received negative reviews in the magazine. Another interesting feature is the large presence of material from the US version of the magazine and the amateurishness of the reviews.

> The predominance of reviews of albums by foreign artists and groups, compared to Brazilian ones, was very high. Initially, these reviews were written by critics from the American Rolling Stone. But in recent editions we've noticed that many of them, both about foreign and Brazilian LPs, were written by people who were attentive readers of the publication. This was the case of Jamari Franga - who became a music critic - or Roberto Navarro - who became a television producer and joined the group Esquadrilha da Fumaga in the 1980s (OLIVEIRA, 2011, p. 87).

Despite these problems, the magazine played an important role at the time for being the first to take a closer look at Brazilian rock music and for pointing out trends that would become a reference in Brazilian music in the following years, such as post-tropicalism and rural rock. RSB was discontinued in 1973 due to financial problems that had worsened since its launch. It was reissued in October 2006, now officially by Springer Publishing[6] . In this new version, the magazine has adapted to the new market reality, moved away from the alternative stance and acquired more commercial characteristics, but without losing its provocative vein and its function as a source of information for those who want to consume culture.

The publication aims to be a source of qualified cultural information that is also accessible to young people. Published monthly, RSB stands out for its criticism, reviews and reports. The focus remains on music, especially rock and pop, but the magazine also features covers and articles on other genres. To a lesser extent, there are articles on topics such as politics, cinema, TV, literature, drugs, information technology, religion, sex, behavior, etc. Around 50% of the publication's content is translated from the North American parent company, in accordance with a clause in the contract for use of the brand. This allows national and international issues to coexist, reinforcing a mix of cultures.

Mirian Magalhaes and Daivson dos Santos (2014) point out some important features in the narrative of the new RSB editions, including: the positioning of the publication as an opinion-former, inducing its reader to reflect according to what its editorial line proposes; the personalization of a public figure that establishes identification with the target audience; and the relationship with the elites, which is characterized by the opinion of influential people such as journalists, artists and political leaders about the character in question, or the comparison to them, translating their notoriety. The journalistic genres of opinion, interpretation and entertainment are the most common.

For the authors, the magazine's editorial line can be seen throughout its content, although there is no specific space to present their opinion. In the publication, both established personalities and internet phenomena guide the content.

[6] It belongs to Grupo Spring de Comunicação, a Brazilian company founded in 2004 to publish in-flight magazines and which today has *Rolling Stone Brasil* as its flagship magazine, responsible for around 70% of the Group's turnover (http://www.springcom.com.br/editora/).

In this sense, the focus of the news is almost always on personalization. Music occupies a third of the magazine, while other themes are explored to a lesser extent.

There is a lot of use of literary journalism[7] in the construction of the profiles, which, however, don't usually problematize the characters' positions. "The reporters participate in such an active way that they are like the celebrities they interview, inducing the reader to step into their shoes" (Magalhaes and Santos, 2014, p. 14). The time of the event is a dispensable factor. "Although cultural journalism may anticipate the agenda, especially those covering major events, RSB usually publishes stories that have some connection to past events so that it can put them in context with the present" (Magalhaes and Santos, 2014, p. 14).

2.1 - Criticism according to critics

To better understand how criticism is done and how critics think, interviews were conducted with journalists Andre Aloi, who currently writes reviews for RSB, and Jamari Franga, a critic specializing in rock music, who wrote reviews for the first version of the magazine as a reader.

Aloi started out in journalism working in TV production, then worked in press offices for mayors, city halls and political parties. He entered entertainment journalism with a blog covering concerts, called Aos Cubos, in 2009. In 2011, he joined the Terra portal as music editor and from then on began writing reviews for Rolling Stone, soon after joining the magazine's online editorial team. He currently works as a reporter for the RG website, where he writes about Culture and Lifestyle; he writes about national cinema for Harper's Bazaar magazine; he closes the Culture section of I magazine, at the Iguatemi shopping mall, and has been producing reviews for RS on a permanent basis since the beginning of 2015.

Franga began his career in the international section of Jornal do Brasil in 1978, and started writing about music in 1982, when he was able to follow the emergence of bands that were the foundation of national rock music.

> "I noticed that bands with funny names were appearing in the city, like Paralamas do Sucesso, Kid Abelha e os Aboboras Selvagens, Blitz etc. I went to the editor of Caderno B and suggested a story. He accepted and I started writing about these new rock bands. I didn't

[7] Journalists use literary journalism as a tool to add stylistic features of literature to their profiles, which gives the text a greater wealth of detail.

> intend to be a critic, I thought of myself as a music reporter, but as you go along, you write about the most popular records and you end up becoming a critic."[8]

When talking about the style of his criticism, Aloi agrees with the lack of impartiality in the review, and adds that he does not follow the posture of judge or executioner, pointed out as recurrent by Fernandes (2010).

> "I try to use my knowledge as a way of situating the reader in which direction the artist is going or whether they might like it because of the determining factors. How that music can act in everyday life as a trail for the person or what inspirations may have led the artist to bet on that timbre or texture to compose that material. It's very imaginative: a heavier *groove*; 70s, with influences from the disco era; and more elaborate pop takes us to the 80s. Synthesizers, nineties... and so on. To show the reader that this was done in the past, but that it's taking on new forms and textures".[9]

The journalist also challenges the role of the review as a determining factor in whether or not the public will listen to a particular record or artist. For him, this is an outdated view, since what predominates today is the review as a historical record of the music scene.

> "I'm 30 years old and I used to get up at the crack of dawn on Fridays a decade ago to find out which song Lucio Ribeiro was going to open his column in Folha de S. Paulo with. Or which *indie* artist he was betting would be the *"next big thing"*. Today, our role is more focused on making a historical record and a snapshot of the current musical period in order to have a record. And I'll say it again: the power to elevate an artist or bury someone's musical career is no longer in our hands. Scenes like that Pasquim cartoon that dethroned Elis Regina and generated a bad buzz about her career don't just depend on those who produce content in Culture today. We can even help, as in the recent case of Biel. Information is in everyone's hands because of the internet. With *streaming* services, you are your own critic.[10]

Franga shares the same view and adds that the critic's relationship with the public now takes the form of a debate, an exchange of experiences, because with the growth of internet access and *streaming* services there is no longer the privileged position of the critic in having greater access to cultural products.

---

[8] Jamari Franga, in an interview conducted by email on 4/10/2016. Quotation marks have been inserted in all the interview excerpts used, to differentiate them from bibliographic citations.
[9] Andre Aloi, in an interview conducted by email on 17/10/2016
[10] Idem.

"In the past, a band's CD or LP came out and fans couldn't listen to it without buying it; they could listen to a song on the radio, but not the whole album, and then they would see the opinion of the critic they trusted. Nowadays, the album is soon on Spotify, so you form your own opinion, then you can read the critic, but you can debate with him on equal terms because you've also heard the album. People follow critics with whom they identify, in my case, for example, I specialize in rock music. They agree or disagree, but they know they're talking to people who like the same thing. In the past, you had to send letters to the editor, which would eventually be published and receive a reply. So the critic today is a partner in the exchange of ideas. They ask what I thought of a certain record and exchange ideas with me."[11]

Aloi says that the style of his reviews has developed in the sense of giving information in a more informal way, closer to a chat with the reader.

"I give information, but with a twist, you know? Not so direct. And that's always been with me. I think this little joke has become a trademark of mine... The other day, my mother sent me a *printout* of an airline magazine with a review of Luiza Possi's album, for example, asking if I had written it. I said no, but the beginning was identical to the beginning of my text in RS, which was: 'Luiza Possi spent half the year in the living room. Pit? No way! She was producing her new album'. Something along those lines... And I thought that the press office could have been inspired by this to write the release."[12]

Another interesting point made by the critic was his transition from newspaper and advisory text to magazine text, pointing out that the latter gives the critic greater freedom to explore the text in an informal way, which also makes it possible to use the techniques of literary journalism pointed out by Magalhaes and Santos (2014).

"When I started working for Bazaar, the editor was Lucio Ribeiro (yes, the guy I used to read in college). My first text went back and forth with adjustments a thousand times. I joked with him that I felt rusty (even though it was my first time writing for a magazine). And he told me something that I still remember today: 'You're writing like a newspaper, straight through. Magazines have the chance to take your style on a journey. Take advantage of that! And in that time, I learned something else: always have a theory about something in the text to hook the reader. I've been betting on that![13]

Franca also follows a very informal style of criticism and says that what sets

[11] Jamari Franca, in an interview with the author.
[12] Andre Aloi, in an interview with the author.
[13] Idem.

him apart is his focus on the technical side of the artist or product in question, something that goes beyond the usual standard of critics in general. "I like to focus on various aspects of a show or album, a side that I like and few colleagues do is talk about the technical side, mixing, instruments used, the performance of the musicians."[14]

Both critics agree that the difference between the reviews in RS and those in other outlets lies more in the language than in the editorial focus. Franga points out that on his blog he has the freedom to use more informal language, with slang and swear words, something that would be more difficult in outlets like RS, which follow a standard and an editorial manual. Aloi explains that working for several media outlets helps him build a stronger relationship with the artists and contributes to getting more information and increasing his background.

> "At RG, I have more freedom because my editor trusts me and I do all the music stuff (from the Aposta column, where I talk about new artists, to the accreditation of concerts and the management of interviews). And at I, in Iguatemi, the scheme is the same as at RS: I use my background and experience of listening to a record or watching a movie and what the lyrics or stories tell us to relate to our daily lives."[15]

In his relationship with his publishers, Franga says that the problems he faced were more to do with the language of his text than its analysis.

> "Yes, I did have problems at Jornal do Brasil, where I was warned several times for using ironies and light words like shit. In 2006, at Globo Online, I got a blog that allowed for lighter language, but there were still rules."[16]

Aloi doesn't encounter any problems and stresses that he has complete confidence in the magazine's editors (he even says that the text doesn't come back to him after editing). He always deals with the editors by email. "I send them the suggestions for the month, they come back with what they've approved and I have a few days to get back to them with the final text."[17]

Both critics analyze the musical genres with which they most identify. Franga writes only about rock and Aloi about pop music, which is his greatest source of knowledge, having lived through an era of great effervescence in the genre (between

---

14 Jamari Franga, in an interview with the author.
15 Andre Aloi, in an interview with the author.
16 Jamari Franga, in an interview with the author.
17 Andre Aloi, in an interview with the author.

the end of the 1990s and 2000s). Aloi also writes about new artists, because he enjoys discovering new bands and sounds, as well as the commercial appeal. "You know when you get goosebumps when you hear a new song and think: is it going to be a hit or does it look like a single? No false modesty, I have a good ear for that," he said. He assures us that he doesn't have any problems with publishers when it comes to dealing with the genre; what's more complicated is the relationship with the artists' fans. The case he cites below serves as an example of how criticism promotes interaction between musicians, readers and journalists.

> "Once, I remember writing a review saying that a Britney Spears album wasn't that good... then the publisher put in the fine line: "the songs aren't bad" and the fans came after me on social media... That was in 2012. If that were the case today, I'd have NeydeCamp on my doorstep to tell me off (laughs). But there was never any censorship. I'm completely free to write: it's my experience of listening to an album."[18]

When making their evaluations, both journalists emphasize the subjective nature of criticism and seem to follow the intention of fulfilling the function of questioning and problematizing in a constructive way, both for the public and for the artists, as indicated by Schoenherr (2005). Franga focuses on the evaluation based on the contextualization of the reviewed work with what has already been produced by the artist and with what already exists in the music scene.

> "A comparison is made between the new album and the old ones, whether there has been progress, whether the band has repeated itself, whether the lyrics are good or just uninspired with rhyming tricks, like "anyway", "so", "me", or rhymes with verbs, which is very easy and indicates that it's not a real inspiration. If it's a new band, you look at their influences, how personal their style is or whether they're repeating the style of another band, which is quite common in beginner bands. Then we assess whether, even by imitating, they are able to make a name for themselves. How do you know all this? From experience, I've been listening to rock music for 54 years, so I have a lot of baggage that I use to analyze bands. It's essential to have a good knowledge of the musical genre you're working with."[19]

Aloi explains how he uses RS's star rating scheme and focuses on analyzing the album as a whole, looking at the coherence of the tracks, how they relate to the music scene as a whole, what they say about the artist in question and his

---

[18] Ditto

[19] Jamari Franga, in an interview with the author.

performance on each one.

> "At RS, I've never given an artist a bad rating. My worst rating was two stars (when the album has few songs that contain a story or are in context with the current music scene). 3 stars is for when the album is average. There's less fuss and more good tones. 3 and a half, I believe, is when the compositions have more to say, and there's always that song in the back of your mind. Four: when it has all the makings of a classic, but slips in one track or another that doesn't fit in with the rest. And 5 are the classics: just right, without changing anything."[20]

As you can see, the two journalists interviewed eschew the figure of the critic as someone who will determine what is good or bad on the cultural scene. Their stance is that of someone who, in the midst of today's vast cultural production, analyzes music from a different perspective, highlighting the products that stand out and deserve a closer look and, at the same time, generating a constructive debate between the public, critics and artists about the whole context of today's music scene. Thus, they fit in with some aspects of the concepts presented by Melo (2003) and Oliveira (2011).

2.2 - Results of the content analysis

For this analysis, four issues were selected between February and May 2016 (Nos. 114, 115, 116 and 117), because they were recent issues, guaranteeing the timeliness of the results, and because of the high number of reviews on Brazilian music.

In addition to interviews, profiles and reports, the current version of Rolling Stones Brasil has the following sections focused on music: Rock & Roll, with news from the alternative music scene and pop culture in general. Discography, which features comments on the work of specific artists or bands, or a selection of outstanding albums from an important genre or movement in pop music; finally, the Guide section, which features reviews of albums, Blu-rays or DVDs, films and books.

In the 'Guide' section, you can see that the reviews follow the American pattern. They all include a contextualization of the work in the artist's career, an analysis of its main characteristics and a conclusion with the critic's general

---

20 Andre Aloi, in an interview with the author.

impression of the product in question. It can also be seen that the reviews have a sober tone. There is no authoritarian, judgmental approach or centrality in the figure of the critic, which is also facilitated by the variety of critics taking part.

The attitude of not applying an incisive and decisive judgment, described by Andre Aloi, seems to be shared by other critics and editors. The reviews tend to value the positive points more than the negative ones of the work in question, although the flaws are also pointed out. The evaluations are done using stars: at the bottom of the section there is a legend explaining the meaning of each grade (5 stars - classic, 4 stars - excellent, 3 stars - good, 2 stars - fair, 1 star - bad) and that the rankings are supervised by the magazine's editors. The table below gives an overview of the reviews analyzed.

Table 1 - Quantitative analysis of reviews published in RSB

Edition	Brazilian artists reviewed	Critical	Evaluation	Seal	Genre
N° 114 Feb./2016	Lobao	Jose Flavio Junior	3 and a half stars	Tratore	Rock
	Wild Law Seekers	Andre Aloi	3 stars	Independent	Pop. Rock
	Almir Sater and Renato Teixeira	Mauro Ferreira	3 stars	Universal Music	Sertanejo raiz/ Folk-Country
	Lara and the Ultralights	Editors	3 stars	Independent	Jazz/MPB
	Da no Couro	Editors	3 stars	Independent	MPB
	Weather	Mauro Ferreira	3 stars	YB Music	MPB
N° 115 Mar./2016	Joao Donato	Jose Flavio Junior	4 stars	Sesc Seal	MPB
	Paulo Ricardo	Mauro Ferreira	3 stars	Universal Music	Pop. Rock
	Ricardo Viginini and Ze	Jose Flavio Junior	3 and a half stars	Tratore	Rural rock
	Chico Salem	Jose Julio do Espirito Santo	3 stars	Independent	MBP/Pop

	Luiz Tati	Mauro Ferreira	4 stars	Dabliu Discos	MPB
N° 116 Apr./2016	Sky	Bruna Veloso	4 stars	Slap	MPB/Pop
	Rashid	Jose Flavio Junior	3 stars	Independent	Hip. Hop
	Urban Legion	Mauro Ferreira	4 stars	Universal Music	Rock
	Luiza Possi	Andre Aloi	3 stars	Independent	Pop
	Pio Lobato	Jose Flavio Junior	3 stars	Discosaoleo	MBP/ Instrumental
	Mundo Livre S/A	Lucas Breda	3 stars	Green Coconut Tree	Hose-Bit
N° 117 May/2016	Zeca Baleiro	Jose Flavio Junior	3 and a half stars	Free Sound	MPB/Pop
	Romulo Froes	Mauro Ferreira	4 stars	Sesc Seal	Samba
	Igor Prado	Editors	3 stars	Independent	Blues
	Autoramas	Jose Flavio Junior	3 stars	HeartsBleed Blue	Rock
	Ed Mota	Itamar Montalvao	3 and a half stars	Lab 344	Soul/Jazz
	Mahmundi	Jose Flavio Junior	4 stars	Stereo Mono	Pop
	Rico Dalasam	Andre Aloi	3 and a half stars	Independent	Hip. Hop/Pop

All the works in the four issues analyzed were rated as good or excellent (3 to 4 stars). This indicates that the magazine and the critics are trying to balance the tone of their texts and shows that there is a change in the role of criticism and in the relationship with the public. It is important to note the similarity in the critics' evaluations, a reflection of the supervision carried out by the magazine's editors, and an indication that they follow an editorial manual.

2.2.1 The appreciation of established artists in the Brazilian music scene

The first page of the section is reserved for the most important line-ups, which are either established artists or up-and-coming names (Lobao, Joao Donato, Cëu and Zeca Baleiro). The text is always more detailed, with more in-depth contextualization and evaluation. It's possible to see that in this text the critic's personality is more evident. In the three reviews produced by Josë Flavio Junior (Lobao, Joao Donato and Zeca Baleiro), it can be seen that he uses a tone of reverence for the artists' legacy, something that also weighs heavily when he looks at the work being reviewed. The review of Joao Donato's album is where this attitude is most evident.

> *Imagine a musician who played in the early days of bossa nova, working with Tom Jobim and Joao Gilberto in the 1950s. Who, in the following decade, helped spread Brazilian sounds abroad, playing with international jazz and Latin music stars. That he returned to Brazil in the 1970s, directed Gal Costa's show and wrote MPB gems with Gilberto Gil, Caetano Veloso and Marcos Valle. That he spent the following years being worshipped and asked to share moments with Martinho da Vila, Marisa Monte and Marcelo D2. Now, be thankful that this musician is not a figment of your imagination and that he lives at the same time as you, playing concerts and releasing records. It's true that Joao Donato's last album was 15 years old. But he never stopped. A myth can very well slow down, live off the glories of the past. But the 81-year-old pianist, born in Acre, is like Bob Dylan: he prefers to be on the road, producing, active. In Donato Eletrico, the plug goes from 110 to 220. Surrounded by musicians who have lived an average of half a century less than him, Donato offers the poor mortals a neat instrumental album that can be compared to the two psychedelic classics he released in the 1970s: A Bad Donato (1970) and Donato/Deodato (1972). The group responsible for making Donato so connected is mostly from São Paulo. On the CD are members of Bixiga 70, musicians who accompany Ceu and Tulipa Ruiz, and even Mauro Refosco, percussionist for the Red Hot Chili Peppers. In total, 25 instrumentalists spread out over the ten songs of Donato Eletrico, always reverent of "Donatian" conventions, but never so shy as not to venture into responsible solos. Douglas Antunes' (Bixiga 70) trombone on the afrofunk "Urbano" is chilling; Richard Fermino's (Patife Band) clarone on "Resort", Donato's favorite track on the album, is a real highlight. The master, of course, shines brightest. As well as letting his fingers loose on electric pianos and various organs, Donato appears in whispers and breaths here and there, adding charm to the journey. A good set of headphones is essential to enjoy "Tartaruga" and find the exact time when the acriano gaiato murmurs the animal's name, accompanied by Cuca Ferreira's flute. A string quartet gives a solemn tone to some of the material (especially when the arrangement is by Laercio de Freitas, the other veteran in the crowd - who also deserved a solo album with*

the same care). But the high spirits and banter end up prevailing, just the way Donato likes it (JUNIOR, 2016, no. 115, p75) .[21]

The language used is very informal and gives the text the tone of an intimate conversation with the reader, a chat between friends. This feature is used by the journalist as an instrument to bring the veteran musician closer to the young audience, which is the majority of the magazine and often has no knowledge of the work of musicians who, like Donato, are far from the mainstream media.

Mauro Ferreira analyzes the album by Paulo Ricardo (Novo álbum), a singer and songwriter of great relevance in national pop, mainly due to his career with the rock band RPM (acronym for Revolugoes por Minuto) in the 1980s. Here the critic observes that, although the artist no longer has the same space in the media, he still maintains his creativity and a loyal audience, characteristics that are generally considered more important by the magazine's approach than mass success.

> *The main artisan of Brazilian techno-pop in the 1980s, Paulo Ricardo is now pursuing a solo career with a sound far removed from the atmosphere of the band that became a mass phenomenon in 1986. Novo Album has the task of putting the artist back on the scene, with ironic titles and the first song chosen to promote the album, "Novo Single", a metalinguistic rock song about the changes in the music market. In a crop of unreleased songs composed with recent partners such as Joao Paulo Mendonqa and Marcos Zeeba, the artist echoes rock traditions, but resorts to ballads, in tune with the more behaved phase of his life. Made for the artist's daughter, "Isabella" is the ballad that serenades the album with the folk touch of the guitars. The song "Eu & Voce (O x da Questao)" declares love without fear of clichés. But the festive atmosphere of "Como Voce" and "Juntos", a song supported by DJ FTampa's electronic beat, signals that Paulo is also looking for other sounds. Between the languid psychedelia of "Sexy" and the re-recording of a theme from the short-lived parallel project PR-5 ("Raio- X", from 2004), Novo Album offers encouragement in the soulful chorus that fills out "Vida Nova" without betraying the confidence of the public won by the artist in his solo career* (FERREIRA, 2016, n°115, p. 76).

2.2.2. The names that make a difference in today's music scene

In the review of singer Cdu's album (Tropix), Bruna Veloso (who is also the magazine's editor-in-chief) puts the artist's entire oeuvre into context, highlighting her ability to reinvent herself with each new work. This ability to reinvent herself is

[21] All the excerpts taken from the magazine texts have been highlighted in italics to differentiate them from the other quotes in the monograph.

also used to make a conversation with the Brazilian music scene in which the composer is inserted, setting Cëu apart from the other artists who emerged along with her in the so-called "new MPB".

> *The soft but striking sound and voice that introduced Ceu to the world in 2005 fooled many skeptics. The mix of references on the debut album of the same name could indicate an artist with "beginner's luck". The mix was competent, but how to keep it going without falling into sameness along the way? Well, Ceu never let herself be victimized by sound traps or the judgment of others. She followed up her debut with Vagarosa (2009), linked to the first CD by the art of mixing well, but distant in the emphasis she gave to reggae and dub. She got it right again. In 2012, with Caravana Sereia Bloom, she added some guitars here, some references to brega there... And, once again, she kept her previous audience, picking up another horde of listeners along the way. This seems to be the São Paulo singer's vocation: to evolve in music as one evolves in life, seeing that the past doesn't come back, but remaining true to herself. And staying true is not synonymous with staying the same. That's why Ceu is a member of that small club of artists who emerged in the 2000s and who, after four albums in a row, have never lost their touch. Tropix, the latest chapter in this journey, reconfigures the singer's work, this time over synthesizers and electronic beats that are sometimes rudimentary, sometimes dancing. "Perfume do Invisivel", the first song, has the same sensuality as "Grains de Beaute" (Vagarosa). "Arrastarte-Ei" has an unabashed swing, carried by the sound of the drumstick in the corner of the drum kit. Ceu makes her collaborators (Pupillo, from Naqao Zumbi, on drums, Lucas Martins, on bass, and the Frenchman HerveSalters, from General Elektriks, on keyboards) take everything in their stride, just like herself. Tropix is Ceu's most electronic album, but it's not only electronic for that reason; it's a work based on drums, bass and effects, which doesn't mean that we don't hear guitars (by Pedro Sa, especially in "Etilica", featuring Tulipa Ruiz) or orchestrated sounds ("Camadas", "Rapsodia Brasilis"). Everyone gives a little of themselves, without affecting it, transforming the album into a soundtrack full of little details to be discovered listen after listen. Two simple treasures: "Sangria", Ceu's poetic partnership with Lira, and the Northeastern salsa of "Minhas Bics". Representing the singer's more pop side is "A Nave Vai", composed by Jorge Du Peixe (Naqao Zumbi). Ceu doesn't reinvent itself in a forced way, just so it doesn't stay the same as it was before: just as you don't end a journey the same way you started it, it's hard for an artist to remain the same, from a human point of view, from one album to the next. The difference between Ceu and the others? She knows how to translate that into sound* (VELOSO, 2016, no. 116, p. 73).

Another way of approaching new music personalities can be seen in Jose

Flavio Junior's review of Mahmundi's debut album. The critic positions the artist on the pop scene, making a reference to the past, associating the image of the newcomer with that of Marina Lima, one of the great names of national pop (the relationship with the elites, observed by Magalhaes and Santos, in this case, the musical elites). This same association *is* used to demonstrate the changes in the phonographic market and the lack of variety in the music that is in evidence on radio and television (essentially sertanejo universitario, pagode and funk), when he quotes at the end of the text an excerpt from Marina's song "Pra Comegar".

> *No analysis of the debut album by the 29-year-old singer, guitarist and drummer from Rio de Janeiro, Marcela Vale, will escape comparisons with the work of Marina Lima. Mahmundi, the alias she has used since the beginning of the decade, coexists well with the shadow, already duly delineated on the EPs Efeito das Cores (2012) and Setembro (2013). The connection between the two is due to the combination of analog and electronic elements and the interest in both blatant pop and sparse ballads. Half of the album's ten tracks, produced by the artist herself, have already been released. But the new versions are more sophisticated, with a clear improvement in the vocal register (see "Quase Sempre"). As seductive as the retreads "Calor do Amor" and "Desaguar", "Eterno Verao" and "Meu Amor" have the potential to expand Marcela's popularity. It remains to be seen whether she will be featured in the opening of a soap opera or whether she will find a place on FMs, something that was fundamental to Marina's success. It's better not to count on those little things from the Old World* (Junior, 2016, n°117, p. 74).

It is clear from the magazine's editions that the intention is to get away from the type of music that dominates the hegemonic media and to seek originality. The vast majority of artists reviewed *are* from alternative and independent labels. When there is the presence of a major label (Som livre, Universal Music and Slap), it is to highlight established names (Legiao Urbana, Paulo Ricardo, Zeca Baleiro). In this respect, the "RS Ouviu" box produced by the editors is noteworthy (only the one for issue 115 was written by Jose Flavio Junior). It's a space where you can see the intention to give visibility to new independent bands or artists who have a different profile or the so-called "something more". Criticism, in this case, still performs the function described by Schoenherr (2005) of selecting and showing the public what is new and different in the music scene. This is what happens in the box with the groups Lara e os Ultraleves and Da no Couro.

Figure 1 - A brief review of the novelties selected by RSB

RS OUVIU

Os grupos Lara e os Ultraleves e Dá no Couro se pautam pelo ecletismo

■ A cantora Laura Aufranc é a criadora do projeto **Lara e os Ultraleves**. Depois de tocar covers de jazz e soul na noite de São Paulo, a banda refinou o som e se preparou para gravar o álbum de estreia. Em *Boa Hora* (independente, ★★★) Laura e seus músicos se mostram versáteis e juntam jazz com MPB. "Take Me with You" é o primeiro single.

Laura: jazz e MPB

■ O grupo carioca **Dá no Couro** mistura música experimental e arte cênica. Em *Cores do Brasil* (independente, ★★★), a trupe faz releituras de clássicos da música popular e cânticos do folclore brasileiro. Os arranjos especiais juntam 18 vozes, violão, baixo e percussão. "Casa Forte" (Edu Lobo), "Caxangá" (Milton Nascimento e Fernando Brant) e "Fantasia" (Chico Buarque) estão entre as faixas do repertório.

Source: Rolling Stone Brasil magazine (n°114, 2016, p. 90)

In the four issues analyzed, Andre Aloi wrote three reviews, in which the style he described in the interview is very evident. His language is very light and figurative, and applies mainly to independent artists and bands that have commercial potential, but are also relevant on the cultural scene. As in the review of Selvagens a Procura da Lei (Praieiro), in which he says that the group is "ready to conquer the radio" and mentions the politicized message present in some of the songs. In the review of the debut album (Orgunga) by rapper Rico Dalasam (2016, no. 117, p. 74), he takes the same approach and also comments on the artist's influences of oriental rhythms and his relevance in giving visibility to black and LGBT culture.

Figure 2 - Debut album review

ESTREIA

Rico Dalasam insere sons indianos e do Oriente Médio no rap

■ Em *Orgunga* (independente, ★★★½), **Rico Dalasam** parece ter cruzado o oceano e aportado na Índia. As inusitadas texturas de flautas e acordes distorcidos, que se assemelham ao som do tambura, situam a cruzada temperada com sintetizadores e beats que sopram da capoeira. É fácil imaginar que algumas faixas, como "Vambora", poderiam muito bem se encaixar em uma coreografia de filmes bollywoodianos. O representante do chamado movimento queer rap aposta também em timbres de brasilidade contemporânea, mas com aspirações monumentais. Em "Dalasam", "Milimili" e "Esse Close Eu Dei" ele se expressa com ainda mais desenvoltura em comparação ao primeiro EP, *Modo Diverso*. Com resquícios da disco music e do groove dos anos 1970, "Nortes" o ratifica como cantor e não apenas como MC. "A cada vez que você diz adeus, você se torna mais livre", ele versa em "Relógios", faixa com guitarra e bateria bem marcadas. Letras espertas e muitas vezes irônicas narram a ascensão de Dalasam na música, ao passo que contos amorosos endossam o significado de "orgunga", expressão criada pelo artista e que sintetiza orgulho negro e gay. ANDRÉ ALOI

Dalasam chega para renovar

Source: Rolling Stone Brasil magazine (n°117, 2016, p. 74)

2.2.3. A non-obvious take on traditional Brazilian products

Mauro Ferreira was responsible for reviewing classic names from the national rock scene (Paulo Ricardo and Legiao Urbana), but his reviews in RS are mainly divided between artists more linked to MPB. The review of the joint album by Almir Sater and Renato Teixeira (AR), musicians whose work is commonly classified by the media as sertanejo raiz or caipira music, is noteworthy. Ferreira distances the two veterans from today's more pop sertanejo and highlights the participation of a North American producer to classify the duo's work as Brazilian folk with a *country* touch.

> *Dissociated from the world of sertanejo pop, Almir Sater and Renato Teixeira unite voices and songs in their first album recorded as a duo. The production by North American Eric Silver has given a country touch to the Brazilians' native folk. This is evident in "D de Destino. But Sater and Teixeira don't change the course of their work. Sater exalts rural life in "Peixe Frito". Teixeira poeticizes passion in "Love Has Many Ways. AR harmonizes the sound and voices of*

singers with similar trajectories (Ferreira, 2016, no. 114, p. 90).

Samba is another genre treated differently by RS. In his review of the album by musician Romulo Froes, Ferreira highlights the experimental character the artist gave to Nelson Cavaquinho's repertoire, distancing himself from the established samba singer's style and giving another interpretation to his work.

> *Romulo Froes has released albums based on noise and dissonance. It is on this experimental route that the artist follows Nelson Cavaquinho's funereal block. Death is the subject of several of the 14 songs sung by Froes with guitars, cymbals and brass that deviate from the cadence of the samba. A classic recorded with Criolo's voice, "Luz Negra" is the apex of the deconstruction, while Na Ozzetti gives voice to the verses created by Nuno Ramos for the samba-choro "Caminhando". At the end, Froes moves through Cavaquinho's morbid universe, far from reverence* (Ferreira, 2016, n° 117, p. 72).

3.2.4. Tackling products with less commercial potential

With a smaller space and a more succinct text are products with a lower commercial profile. Tcзё Julio do Espirito Santo analyzes the second album by multi-instrumentalist Chico Salem (Maior ou Igual a Dois), and highlights the musician's evolution, putting him in context alongside big names, when he mentions the legacy he has made over the years working with singer-songwriter Arnaldo Antunes (here, once again, the relationship with the musical elites is made).

> *In this second solo album, Salem has come a long way from his debut, 01 (2002). Friends made over a career spanning more than two decades - much of that time as the guitarist in Arnaldo Antunes' band - are present. "Num Dia" grows in a kind of Caribbean wall of sound provided by Bixiga 70. "Um Fio" features Karina Buhr sharing the vocals with Salem* (Santo, 2016, no. 115, p. 77).

Itamar Montalvao reviewed Ed Motta's album Perpetual Gateways. He views the album's ten tracks as a unit and sees in it the maturity that the musician has achieved throughout his career, making music that the journalist classifies as refined. The album is based on soul and jazz, the latter a genre considered more elaborate and aimed at a more restricted audience.

> *With a devotion to his influences, Ed Motta brings back the concept of the LP Perpetual Gateways, divided into two sides. Side A, which he calls*

"Soul Gate", begins with "Captain's Refusal" and "Hypochondriac's Fun", which exude a classy mix of rock and funk and are reminiscent of Steely Dan, a great reference point for Motta. On the B-side, called "Jazz Gate", Motta takes the band by the hand and sets off on a journey through intricate paths that lead to spirit jazz and fusion, until the apotheotic ending with "Overblown Over-weight". Listening to the ten tracks, you get the impression that he has been maturing to culminate in the refined music he made in this work (Montalvao, 2016, no. 117, p. 73).

Lucas Breda was responsible for the review of the live album by the group Icone, from the Mangue-Bit movement Mundo Livre S/A. He focuses on the performance of the musicians and the instruments used (similar to Jamari Franga's style), highlights the band's influential style and cites the absence of songs from the repertoire of the first album as a flaw. Mangue-Bit is a movement with a genuinely popular origin and theme, but which over the years has been restricted to a specific niche due to its more artistic nature.

After eight studio albums, the Pernambucans revisit live songs from the group's three decades of existence. Wielding the cavaquinho, Fred Zero Quatro leads the band in a full-bodied configuration (including brass), ideal for songs like "Meu Esquema". However, this leaves older tracks like "Livre Iniciativa" and "Computadores Fazem Arte" more subdued. A fair portrayal of Mundo Livre S/A's influential aesthetic, Ao Vivo slips up by leaving out the band's first and seminal album, Samba Esquema Noise (only one track was included in its entirety on the CD, while the DVD features more performances from the album) (Breda, 2016, n° 116, p. 75).

3 - Conclusions

In the classical conception, criticism, as a journalistic genre, would be the main means of selecting what was good or bad in the music industry. The critic would be someone with greater access to cultural products, able to make this selection and also present to the public what is not within their reach.

However, the role of the critic is changing. With the advance of digital technologies and changes in the music industry, the public has had increasing access to a variety of music and artists, causing a transformation in their relationship with criticism and critics. Now the public searches for itself what to listen to and goes to the critic to compare the experiences and evaluations that have been made about a certain product, generating greater interaction and a more active debate in the critic-musician-public relationship.

Rolling Stone Brasil magazine is part of this scenario of transformations in the cultural industry. In its criticism section, it establishes, through the plurality of journalists who write the reviews, a demystification of the figure of the critic. There is no one name that stands out or has the power to make an incisive judgment. The personality of the critic in the text is very diluted, and although the analysis is subjective, it follows a pattern that allows for a balanced approach. These characteristics, together with the absence of negative evaluations, show that the time of the review with exalted opinions and critics with a strong personalization of their image, which marked the first version of the magazine, has passed.

In the magazine's criticism, the three basic functions pointed out by Fernandes (2010) are present - guidance for readers, discussion and helping the artist to evaluate their work. It can also perform the function pointed out by Fenster (2002), of answering the reader whether or not they should listen to that record, although this is not its only role. Reviews mainly have the function of providing a historical context, relating the work to what was produced in the past, always revering the great names, and to what is currently being done. In this sense, they can promote a social reading of the musical production of an era and are therefore outside the "de-intellectualization" pointed out by the first author.

The magazine caters to an audience that doesn't prefer the Brazilian genres that are so popular in today's media. As such, it relates to what escapes this dominant trend and aims to highlight personalities who have an originality, who bring something new, or a different interpretation of what is new.

that has already been done, without sacrificing the artist's identity. Commercial value is important and is what gets the most attention in "Guia", but experimental works or those with a more artistic value also get space. Rock continues to be widely debated, but it no longer seems to be the magazine's main protagonist. Pop music and MPB have gained a lot of space and coexist on an equal footing with the genre that gave rise to the publication.

We can conclude, through the case of RS, that criticism plays a journalistic role which, although in the process of changing, still influences the cultural industry and has the capacity to promote an exchange of ideas, generate debate, give visibility to new productions that don't meet the standards of the major labels and record companies, but which have a potential for originality and give a freshness to the Brazilian music scene, which, being very vast and rich in influences and sounds, should be explored with attention, without focusing exclusively on the obvious.

4 - Bibliography

BOLLOS, Liliana Harb. **Music criticism in the newspaper: a reflection on Brazilian culture.** ANPOOM Opus, v. 11, p. 147-58, 2004.

DUARTE, Jorge. BARROS, Antonio (orgs). **Metodos e Tecnicas de Pesquisa em Comunicagao.** 2ª Edition, Sao Paulo: Atlas, 2009.

ENCICLOPEDIA Intercom de Comunicação Sao Paulo: Sociedade Brasileira de Estudos Interdisciplinares da Comunicação, 2010. 1 v.

FERNANDES, Fernanda Pires Alvarenga. **Criticism and crisis in the cultural section:** an analysis of the main national periodicals. 2010. Paper presented at the VIII National Meeting of Journalism Researchers, Federal University of Maranhao, Sao Luis, November 2010.

GOLBSPAN, Heloisa. Analise de Conteudo In: **Metodologia de pesquisa em jornalismo.** 2a Edigao, Rio de Janeiro: Editora Vozes, 2007, 124 p.

MAGALHAES, Mirian MM; Dos SANTOS, Daivson Pereira. **Journalistic genres, newsworthiness criteria and new journalism:** an analysis of Rolling Stone Brasill magazine. 2014. Paper presented at the XXXVII Brazilian Congress of Communication Sciences, Foz do Iguagu, PR, September 2014.

MELO, Josd Marques de. **Jornalismo Opinativo: Opinionated** genres in Brazilian journalism. Campos do Jordao: Mantiqueira, 2003.

OLIVEIRA, Cassiano Francisco Scherner de. **Brazilian rock criticism in magazine journalism specialized in sound, music and youth:** from Rolling Stone (1972-1973) to Bizz (1985-2001). Porto Alegre. PUCRS, 2011, 381p Thesis (Doctorate in Communication) - by the Postgraduate Program in Communication of the Pontifical Catholic University of Rio Grande do Sul.

SALDANHA, Rafael Machado. **Rock em revista:** rock journalism in Brazil. Juiz de Fora: UFJF, p. 1-15, 2005.

SCHOENHERR, Rafael. **Journalism as (potentially polemical) feedback on music in the age of media culture.** 2005. Paper presented at the III National Meeting of Journalism Researchers, Florianopolis - SC, November 2005.

ANNEXES

A. Interviews

From: Jamari Franca - **Sent:** 3/10/2016 - **Replied**: 4/10/2016

1 - What was your career path before and during your work as a critic?

I joined Jornal do Brasil in November 1978 for the international section. I only started writing about music in October 1982. I noticed that bands with funny names were appearing in the city, such as Paralamas do Sucesso, Kid Abelha e os Aboboras Selvagens, Blitz etc. I went to the editor of Caderno B and suggested an article. He accepted and I started writing about these new rock bands. I didn't intend to be a critic, I thought of myself as a music reporter, but as you go along, you start writing about legendary records and end up becoming a critic.

2 - How do you define the style of your criticism?

I like to focus on various aspects of a show or album, a side that I enjoy and few colleagues do, and talk about the technical side, the mix, the instruments used, the performance of the musicians.

3 - Does your style vary according to the medium you're writing for?

In newspapers it was a more serious style, with more formal vocabulary according to the rules of the medium. Nowadays, on my blog, it's very loose language, including slang and swear words.

4 - Do you notice any differences between RS Brasil's criticism and that of other media?

They are all in the same style as I mentioned, with the language that the media outlet allows, and they all have a writing manual that the journalist must follow.

5 - Which genre do you most like to criticize, or which do you most identify with, and how free are you to deal with it?

I only write about rock, I specialize in it.

6 - How did you develop your style? Have you ever had any problems with editors?

My style has always been very informal. I did get into trouble at Jornal do Brasil for using a few ironies and light words, like "shit", and I was warned several times. In 2006, I got a blog at Globo Online that allowed me to use lighter language, but there were still rules.

7 - What are your criteria for saying whether the object of criticism is good or bad?

It depends. Criticism always has a subjective side, it's easier if you identify with the band. But a comparison between the new album and the old ones is taken into account, whether there has been progress, whether the band has repeated itself, whether the lyrics are good or just uninspired with rhyming tricks like "at last", "so", "me" or rhymes with verbs, which is very easy and indicates that there is no real inspiration. If it's a new band, you look at its influences, how personal its style is or whether it's repeating the style of another band, which is even common in beginner bands, and then you assess whether it's capable of making a name for itself, even if it's imitating. How do you know all this? From experience, I've been listening to rock music for 54 years, so I have a lot of baggage that I use to analyze bands. It's essential to have a good knowledge of the musical genre you're working with.

Follow-up question asked on 18/10/2016.

8 - Do you agree that criticism is no longer a determining factor in whether or not a person will listen to a certain record or artist? What is the role of music criticism today?

Criticism no longer plays the same role because today people have access to it. For example. In the past, a band's CD or LP came out and the band's fans couldn't listen to it without buying it, they could listen to a song on the radio, but not the whole album, and then they would see the opinion of the critic they trusted. Nowadays, the album is soon on Spotify, so you can form your own opinion, then you can read the reviewer, but you can debate with them as equals because you've also heard the album. People follow critics with whom they identify, in my case, for example, who specialize in rock, it's those who like rock. They agree or disagree, but they know they're talking to people who like the same thing. In the past, you had to send letters to the editor, which would eventually be published and receive a reply. So the critic today is a partner in the exchange of ideas. They ask what I thought of a certain record and exchange ideas with me.

From: Andre Aloi

Submitted: 15/10/2016 - **Responded**: 17/10/2016

1 - What was your career path before and during your work as a critic?

I started out in journalism, working in TV production. I then worked as a press officer (for a long time I was an advisor to mayors, city councils and political parties). I fell into entertainment journalism because I set up a concert coverage blog called Aos Cubos in 2009. In 2011, I worked for the Terra portal as a music reporter (during which time I wrote my first reviews for Rolling Stone), and then I worked in the online section of Quem magazine at Globo. I went on to work producing content for artists and festivals, as well as brands that used music as a platform for talking to their audiences. Two years ago, I worked as a reporter for the RG website, where I wrote about culture and lifestyle. At Harper's Bazaar magazine, my focus is national cinema. I've been writing for Rolling Stone on a regular basis since the beginning of 2015, and I also close the Culture section of I magazine, in the Iguatemi shopping mall.

2 - How do you define the style of your criticism?

I don't know if it's possible to be impartial (because we give a grade and say whether it's good or bad), but I try not to be a blowhard. I think the figure of the guy who points the finger in the artist's face with his arrogance is a thing of the past. I try to use my knowledge as a way of situating the reader in which direction the artist is going or whether they might like it because of the determining factors. How that music might act in everyday life as a track for the person or what inspirations might have led the artist to bet on that timbre or texture to compose that material. It's very imaginative: a heavier groove: 70s, with influences from the disco era and more elaborate pop takes us back to the 80s. Synthesizers, nineties... and so on. Showing the reader that this was done in the past, but that it's taking on new forms and textures. Criticism won't be a determining factor in whether or not a person listens to a certain record or artist, as it was with my generation, for example. I'm 30 years old and I used to get up at the crack of dawn on Fridays a decade ago to find out which song Lucio Ribeiro was going to open his column with in Folha de S. Paulo. Or which indie artist he was betting would be the "next big thing". Today, our role is more focused on making a historical record and a snapshot of the current musical period in order to have a record. And I'll say it again: the power to elevate an artist or bury someone's musical career is no longer in our hands. Scenes like that Pasquim cartoon that dethroned Elis Regina and generated a bad wave about her career don't just depend on those who produce content in Culture today. We can even help, as in the recent case of Biel. Information is in everyone's hands because of the internet. With streaming services, you are your own critic.

3 - What's the difference between your criticism in Rolling Stone and in other media?

The language changes, but the editorial focus is practically the same - despite the audience. It's happened, for example, that I've done an "In Studio" for RS and then written a review of an album. Then, a few weeks later, I had to interview the artist for a feature in Radar or Bazaar. This strengthens the bond with the artist and increases the chances of getting exclusive information or an interview without restrictions. At RG, I have more freedom because my editor trusts me and I do all the music stuff (from the Aposta column, where I talk about new artists, to the accreditation of concerts and the management of interviews). And at I, in Iguatemi, the scheme is the same as at RS: I use my background and experience of listening to a record or watching a movie and what the lyrics or stories tell us to relate to our daily lives.

4 - Which genre do you most like to criticize, or which do you most identify with, and how free are you to deal with it?

At RS, I basically talk about Pop (which is my greatest source of knowledge, I lived through the golden age of Pop, between the end of the 90's and 00's) and new artists because I love discovering bands and sounds, but again: leaning towards the more commercial. Not that I don't talk about other subjects, but you know when you get goosebumps when you hear a new song and think: is it going to be a hit or does it look like a single? No false modesty, I have a good ear for that. Text adjustments are minimal. Once, I remember writing a review saying that a Britney Spears album wasn't that good... then the publisher put in the fine line: "atd songs that aren't bad" and the fans came after me on social media... That was in 2012. If that were the case today, I'd have NeydeCamp on my doorstep to tell me off (laughs). But there was never any censorship. I have total freedom to write: it's my experience of listening to a certain album.

5 - How did you develop your style?

It's funny that, until recently, I didn't think I had my own style - although ever since college I remember wanting to do the lead with some flair. There was an exercise by a professor I really admired in college. He separated three piles of texts in a lead assessment. Some were incorrect, others were correct. And the third was mine, which was the only correct one. I swear it's not a bragging story, but I think that's where the style thing comes from. I give the information, but with a twist, you know? Not so direct. And that's always been with me. I think this playfulness has become a trademark of mine... The other day, my mother sent me a printout of an airline magazine with a review of Luiza Possi's album, for example, asking if I had written it. I said no, but the beginning was identical to my beginning in the RS text, which was: "Luiza Possi spent half the year in her living room. A cesspit? No way! She was producing her new album". Something along those lines... And I thought that the press office might have been inspired by this to write the press release. And I was always betting on that, even when I was writing press releases. You know when your teacher tells you in college: you have to convince the reader in the lead? I always try to do that! When I started working at Bazaar, the editor was Lucio Ribeiro (yes, the guy I used to read when I was at university). My first text went back and forth with adjustments a thousand times. I joked with him that I felt rusty (even though it was my first time writing for a magazine). And he said something to me that I still remember today: "You're writing like a newspaper, straightforward. Magazines have the chance to take a trip in style. Take advantage of that!". And in that time, I learned something else: always have a theory about something in the text to hook the reader.

I've been betting on it!

6 - How is your relationship with RS editors? Have there ever been any problems?

I've never had any problems. I trust them completely, so much so that the text doesn't even come back to me after editing. And I always deal with them by email. So much so that in the six years I've been talking to Paulo Cavalcanti (editor of Guia), I only met him in person a few weeks ago, at the Wilco concert in São Paulo. A friend gave me his contact details in 2010, when I sent him an email and we talk all the time. I send him the suggestions for the month, he sends back what he's approved and I have a few days to get back to him with the final text.

7 - What are your criteria for saying whether the object of criticism is good or bad?

As I said, it's very subjective to say whether something is good or bad. So much so that Folha recently added more options to define the critique of a show, movie, or film. Now it's no evaluation, bad, regular, good, very good and great. At RS, I've never given a bad rating to an artist. My worst rating was two stars (when the album has few songs that contain a story or contextualize the current music scene). 3 stars is for when the album is average. There's less fuss and more good tones. 3 and a half, I believe, is when the compositions have more to say, there's always that song in the back of your mind. Four: when it has everything it needs to be a classic, but slips in one track or another that doesn't fit in with the rest. And 5 are the classics: just right, without changing anything. But that could also just be a thesis that I've just been trying to figure out in my head. And none of it works in practice (laughs).

B. Covers of the editions analyzed

Issue #114 - February 2016

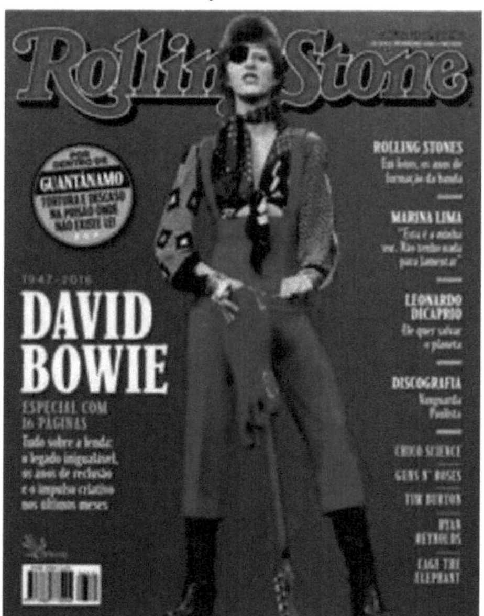

Issue 115 - March 2016

Issue no. 116 - April 2016

Issue no. 117 - May 2016

Printed by Books on Demand GmbH, Norderstedt / Germany